Justice and Security Bill [HL]

EXPLANATORY NOTES

Explanatory notes to the Bill, prepared by the Cabinet Office, Home Office and Ministry of Justice, are published separately as HL Bill 27—EN.

EUROPEAN CONVENTION ON HUMAN RIGHTS

Lord Wallace of Tankerness has made the following statement under section 19(1)(a) of the Human Rights Act 1998:

In my view the provisions of the Justice and Security Bill [HL] are compatible with the Convention rights.

Justice and Security Bill [HL]

CONTENTS

PART 1

OVERSIGHT OF INTELLIGENCE AND SECURITY ACTIVITIES

Oversight by the Intelligence and Security Committee

1. The Intelligence and Security Committee
2. Main functions of the ISC
3. Reports of the ISC
4. Sections 1 to 3: interpretation

Oversight by the Intelligence Services Commissioner

5. Additional review functions of the Commissioner

PART 2

RESTRICTIONS ON DISCLOSURE OF SENSITIVE MATERIAL

Closed material procedure: general

6. Proceedings in which court permits closed material applications
7. Determination by court of applications in section 6 proceedings
8. Appointment of special advocate
9. Saving for normal disclosure rules
10. General provision about section 6 proceedings
11. Sections 6 to 10: interpretation

Closed material procedure: immigration

12. Certain exclusion, naturalisation and citizenship decisions

"Norwich Pharmacal" and similar jurisdictions

13. Disclosure proceedings
14. Review of certification

Part 3

General

15 Consequential and transitional etc. provision
16 Commencement, extent and short title

Schedule 1 — The Intelligence and Security Committee
Schedule 2 — Consequential provision
    Part 1 — Oversight of intelligence and security activities
    Part 2 — Closed material procedure
Schedule 3 — Transitional provision
    Part 1 — Oversight of intelligence and security activities
    Part 2 — Closed material procedure
    Part 3 — "Norwich Pharmacal" and similar jurisdictions

A

BILL

TO

Provide for oversight of the Security Service, the Secret Intelligence Service, the Government Communications Headquarters and other activities relating to intelligence or security matters; to provide for closed material procedure in relation to certain civil proceedings; to prevent the making of certain court orders for the disclosure of sensitive information; and for connected purposes.

BE IT ENACTED by the Queen's most Excellent Majesty, by and with the advice and consent of the Lords Spiritual and Temporal, and Commons, in this present Parliament assembled, and by the authority of the same, as follows:—

PART 1

OVERSIGHT OF INTELLIGENCE AND SECURITY ACTIVITIES

Oversight by the Intelligence and Security Committee

1   The Intelligence and Security Committee

(1) There is to be a body known as the Intelligence and Security Committee (in this Part referred to as "the ISC").

(2) The ISC is to consist of nine members who are to be drawn both from the members of the House of Commons and from the members of the House of Lords.

(3) Each member of the ISC is to be appointed by the House of Parliament from which the member is to be drawn.

(4) A person is not eligible to become a member of the ISC unless the person—
  (a) is nominated for membership by the Prime Minister, and
  (b) is not a Minister of the Crown.

(5) Before deciding whether to nominate a person for membership, the Prime Minister must consult the Leader of the Opposition.

(6) A member of the ISC is to be the Chair of the ISC chosen by its members.

(7) Schedule 1 (which makes further provision about the ISC) has effect.

2 Main functions of the ISC

(1) The ISC may examine or otherwise oversee the expenditure, administration, policy and operations of—
   (a) the Security Service,
   (b) the Secret Intelligence Service, and
   (c) the Government Communications Headquarters.

(2) The ISC may examine or otherwise oversee such other activities of Her Majesty's Government in relation to intelligence or security matters as are set out in a memorandum of understanding.

(3) The ISC may, by virtue of subsection (1) or (2), consider any particular operational matter but only so far as the ISC and the Prime Minister are satisfied that—
   (a) the matter—
      (i) is not part of any ongoing intelligence or security operation, and
      (ii) is of significant national interest, and
   (b) the consideration of the matter is consistent with any principles set out in, or other provision made by, a memorandum of understanding.

(4) A memorandum of understanding under this section—
   (a) may include other provision about the ISC or its functions which is not of the kind envisaged in subsection (2) or (3),
   (b) must be agreed between the Prime Minister and the ISC, and
   (c) may be altered (or replaced with another memorandum) with the agreement of the Prime Minister and the ISC.

(5) The ISC must publish a memorandum of understanding under this section and lay a copy of it before Parliament.

3 Reports of the ISC

(1) The ISC must make an annual report to Parliament on the discharge of its functions.

(2) The ISC may make such other reports to Parliament as it considers appropriate concerning any aspect of its functions.

(3) Before making a report to Parliament, the ISC must send a draft of it to the Prime Minister.

(4) The ISC must exclude any matter from any report to Parliament if the Prime Minister, after consultation with the ISC, considers that the matter would be prejudicial to the continued discharge of the functions of the Security Service, the Secret Intelligence Service, the Government Communications Headquarters or any person carrying out activities falling within section 2(2).

(5) A report by the ISC to Parliament must contain a statement as to whether any matter has been excluded from the report by virtue of subsection (4).

(6) The ISC must lay before Parliament any report made by it to Parliament.

(7) The ISC may make a report to the Prime Minister in relation to matters which would be excluded by virtue of subsection (4) if the report were made to Parliament.

4 Sections 1 to 3: interpretation

In sections 1 to 3 and Schedule 1—

"government department" means a department of Her Majesty's Government but does not include—
  (a) the Security Service,
  (b) the Secret Intelligence Service, or
  (c) the Government Communications Headquarters,

"Her Majesty's forces" has the same meaning as in the Armed Forces Act 2006,

"Her Majesty's Government" means Her Majesty's Government in the United Kingdom,

"Leader of the Opposition" has the same meaning as in the Ministerial and other Salaries Act 1975,

"Minister of the Crown" has the same meaning as in the Ministers of the Crown Act 1975,

"notice" means notice in writing.

Oversight by the Intelligence Services Commissioner

5 Additional review functions of the Commissioner

After section 59 of the Regulation of Investigatory Powers Act 2000 (Intelligence Services Commissioner) insert—

"59A Additional functions of the Intelligence Services Commissioner

(1) So far as directed to do so by the Prime Minister and subject to subsection (2), the Intelligence Services Commissioner must keep under review the carrying out of any aspect of the functions of—
  (a) an intelligence service,
  (b) a head of an intelligence service, or
  (c) any part of Her Majesty's forces, or of the Ministry of Defence, so far as engaging in intelligence activities.

(2) Subsection (1) does not apply in relation to anything which is required to be kept under review by the Interception of Communications Commissioner or under section 59.

(3) The Prime Minister may give a direction under this section at the request of the Intelligence Services Commissioner or otherwise.

(4) Directions under this section may, for example, include directions to the Intelligence Services Commissioner to keep under review the implementation or effectiveness of particular policies of the head of an intelligence service regarding the carrying out of any of the functions of the intelligence service.

(5) The Prime Minister must publish, in a manner which the Prime Minister considers appropriate, any direction under this section (and

any revocation of such a direction) except so far as it appears to the Prime Minister that such publication would be contrary to the public interest or prejudicial to—

 (a) national security,

 (b) the prevention or detection of serious crime,

 (c) the economic well-being of the United Kingdom, or

 (d) the continued discharge of the functions of any public authority whose activities include activities that are subject to review by the Intelligence Services Commissioner.

(6) In this section "head", in relation to an intelligence service, means—

 (a) in relation to the Security Service, the Director-General,

 (b) in relation to the Secret Intelligence Service, the Chief, and

 (c) in relation to GCHQ, the Director."

PART 2

RESTRICTIONS ON DISCLOSURE OF SENSITIVE MATERIAL

Closed material procedure: general

6 Proceedings in which court permits closed material applications

(1) The Secretary of State may apply to the court seised of relevant civil proceedings for a declaration that the proceedings are proceedings in which a closed material application may be made to the court.

(2) The court must, on an application under subsection (1), make such a declaration if the court considers that—

 (a) a party to the proceedings (whether or not the Secretary of State) would be required to disclose material in the course of the proceedings to another person (whether or not another party to the proceedings), and

 (b) such a disclosure would be damaging to the interests of national security.

(3) In deciding whether a party to the proceedings would be required to disclose material, the court must ignore—

 (a) the fact that there would be no requirement to disclose if—

  (i) the material were withheld on grounds of public interest immunity, or

  (ii) the person concerned chose not to rely upon the material, and

 (b) section 17(1) of the Regulation of Investigatory Powers Act 2000 (exclusion for intercept material).

(4) A declaration under this section must identify the party or parties to the proceedings whose disclosure or disclosures the court considers would be damaging to the interests of national security ("a relevant person").

(5) Before making an application under subsection (1), the Secretary of State must consider whether to make, or advise another person to make, a claim for public interest immunity in relation to the material on which the application would be based.

(6) Rules of court may—

(a) provide for notification to the Secretary of State by a party to relevant civil proceedings, or by the court concerned, of proceedings to which a declaration under this section may be relevant,

(b) provide for a stay or sist of relevant civil proceedings (whether on an application by a party to the proceedings or by the court concerned of its own motion) where the Secretary of State is considering whether to apply for a declaration under this section,

(c) provide for the Secretary of State, if not a party to proceedings in relation to which there is a declaration under this section, to be joined as a party to the proceedings.

(7) In this section—

"closed material application" means an application of the kind mentioned in section 7(1)(a),

"relevant civil proceedings" means any proceedings (other than proceedings in a criminal cause or matter) before—
(a) the High Court,
(b) the Court of Appeal, or
(c) the Court of Session.

7 Determination by court of applications in section 6 proceedings

(1) Rules of court relating to any relevant civil proceedings in relation to which there is a declaration under section 6 ("section 6 proceedings") must secure—

(a) that a relevant person has the opportunity to make an application to the court for permission not to disclose material otherwise than to—
  (i) the court,
  (ii) any person appointed as a special advocate, and
  (iii) where the Secretary of State is not the relevant person but is a party to the proceedings, the Secretary of State,

(b) that such an application is always considered in the absence of every other party to the proceedings (and every other party's legal representative),

(c) that the court is required to give permission for material not to be disclosed if it considers that the disclosure of the material would be damaging to the interests of national security,

(d) that, if permission is given by the court not to disclose material, it must consider requiring the relevant person to provide a summary of the material to every other party to the proceedings (and every other party's legal representative),

(e) that the court is required to ensure that such a summary does not contain material the disclosure of which would be damaging to the interests of national security.

(2) Rules of court relating to section 6 proceedings must secure that provision to the effect mentioned in subsection (3) applies in cases where a relevant person—

(a) does not receive the permission of the court to withhold material, but elects not to disclose it, or

(b) is required to provide another party to the proceedings with a summary of material that is withheld, but elects not to provide the summary.

(3) The court must be authorised—
   (a) if it considers that the material or anything that is required to be summarised might adversely affect the relevant person's case or support the case of another party to the proceedings, to direct that the relevant person—
      (i) is not to rely on such points in that person's case, or
      (ii) is to make such concessions or take such other steps as the court may specify, or
   (b) in any other case, to ensure that the relevant person does not rely on the material or (as the case may be) on that which is required to be summarised.

8 Appointment of special advocate

(1) The appropriate law officer may appoint a person to represent the interests of a party in any section 6 proceedings from which the party (and any legal representative of the party) is excluded.

(2) A person appointed under subsection (1) is referred to in this section as appointed as a "special advocate".

(3) The "appropriate law officer" is—
   (a) in relation to proceedings in England and Wales, the Attorney General,
   (b) in relation to proceedings in Scotland, the Advocate General for Scotland, and
   (c) in relation to proceedings in Northern Ireland, the Advocate General for Northern Ireland.

(4) A person appointed as a special advocate is not responsible to the party to the proceedings whose interests the person is appointed to represent.

(5) A person may be appointed as a special advocate only if—
   (a) in the case of an appointment by the Attorney General, the person has a general qualification for the purposes of section 71 of the Courts and Legal Services Act 1990,
   (b) in the case of an appointment by the Advocate General for Scotland, the person is an advocate or a solicitor who has rights of audience in the Court of Session or the High Court of Justiciary by virtue of section 25A of the Solicitors (Scotland) Act 1980, and
   (c) in the case of an appointment by the Advocate General for Northern Ireland, the person is a member of the Bar of Northern Ireland.

9 Saving for normal disclosure rules

Subject to sections 7, 8 and 10, rules of court relating to section 6 proceedings must secure that the rules of disclosure otherwise applicable to those proceedings continue to apply in relation to the disclosure of material by a relevant person.

10 General provision about section 6 proceedings

(1) A person making rules of court relating to section 6 proceedings must have regard to the need to secure that disclosures of information are not made where they would be damaging to the interests of national security.

(2) Rules of court relating to section 6 proceedings may make provision—
   (a) about the mode of proof and about evidence in the proceedings,
   (b) enabling or requiring the proceedings to be determined without a hearing,
   (c) about legal representation in the proceedings,
   (d) enabling the proceedings to take place without full particulars of the reasons for decisions in the proceedings being given to a party to the proceedings (or to any legal representative of that party),
   (e) enabling the court concerned to conduct proceedings in the absence of any person, including a party to the proceedings (or any legal representative of that party),
   (f) about the functions of a person appointed as a special advocate,
   (g) enabling the court to give a party to the proceedings a summary of evidence taken in the party's absence.

(3) In subsection (2) references to a party to the proceedings do not include the relevant person concerned and (if the Secretary of State is not the relevant person but is a party to the proceedings) the Secretary of State.

(4) Proceedings on, or in relation to, an application under section 6(1) are to be treated as section 6 proceedings for the purposes of sections 7 to 9, this section and section 11.

(5) Sections 7 to 9, this section and section 11 apply in relation to proceedings treated as section 6 proceedings by subsection (4) as if the Secretary of State were the relevant person.

11 Sections 6 to 10: interpretation

(1) In sections 6 to 10 and this section—
   "enactment" means an enactment whenever passed or made and includes—
      (a) an enactment contained in this Act,
      (b) an enactment contained in subordinate legislation within the meaning of the Interpretation Act 1978,
      (c) an enactment contained in, or in an instrument made under, an Act of the Scottish Parliament,
      (d) an enactment contained in, or in an instrument made under, Northern Ireland legislation, and
      (e) an enactment contained in, or in an instrument made under, a Measure or Act of the National Assembly for Wales,
   "the Human Rights Convention" means the Convention within the meaning of the Human Rights Act 1998 (see section 21(1) of that Act),
   "relevant civil proceedings" has the meaning given by section 6(7),
   "relevant person" has the meaning given by section 6(4) and includes any person treated as a relevant person by any enactment,
   "section 6 proceedings" has the meaning given by section 7(1) and includes any proceedings treated as section 6 proceedings by any enactment,
   "special advocate" has the meaning given by section 8(2),
and references to a party's legal representative do not include a person appointed as a special advocate.

(2) The Secretary of State may by order amend the definition of "relevant civil proceedings" in section 6(7).

(3) The power to make an order under subsection (2) —
    (a) may, in particular, be exercised so as to add or remove a court or tribunal,
    (b) includes power to make supplementary, incidental, consequential, transitional, transitory or saving provision (including provision amending, repealing or otherwise modifying any enactment),
    (c) is exercisable by statutory instrument which is not to be made unless a draft of the instrument has been laid before, and approved by a resolution of, each House of Parliament.

(4) An order under subsection (2) which adds a tribunal to the definition of "relevant civil proceedings" in section 6(7) may, in particular, amend any provision of sections 6 to 10 and this section for the purpose of —
    (a) explaining the meaning of "rules of court" in relation to a tribunal, and
    (b) requiring or enabling provision of a particular description to be made by such rules of court (including provision, about the composition of a tribunal for the purposes of section 6 proceedings, which disapplies or modifies an enactment).

(5) Nothing in sections 6 to 10 and this section (or in any provision made by virtue of them) —
    (a) restricts the power to make rules of court or the matters to be taken into account when doing so,
    (b) affects the common law rules as to the withholding, on grounds of public interest immunity, of any material in any proceedings, or
    (c) is to be read as requiring a court or tribunal to act in a manner inconsistent with Article 6 of the Human Rights Convention.

Closed material procedure: immigration

12 Certain exclusion, naturalisation and citizenship decisions

After section 2B of the Special Immigration Appeals Commission Act 1997 (appeals against certain deprivation of citizenship decisions) insert —

"2C Jurisdiction: review of certain exclusion decisions

(1) Subsection (2) applies in relation to any direction about the exclusion of a non-EEA national from the United Kingdom which —
    (a) is made by the Secretary of State wholly or partly on the ground that the exclusion from the United Kingdom of the non-EEA national is conducive to the public good,
    (b) is not subject to a right of appeal, and
    (c) is certified by the Secretary of State as a direction that was made wholly or partly in reliance on information which, in the opinion of the Secretary of State, should not be made public —
        (i) in the interests of national security,
        (ii) in the interests of the relationship between the United Kingdom and another country, or
        (iii) otherwise in the public interest.

(2) The non-EEA national to whom the direction relates may apply to the Special Immigration Appeals Commission to set aside the direction.

(3) In determining whether the direction should be set aside, the Commission must apply the principles which would be applied in judicial review proceedings.

(4) If the Commission decides that the direction should be set aside, it may make any such order, or give any such relief, as may be made or given in judicial review proceedings.

(5) In this section—

"non-EEA national" means any person who is not a national of an EEA state,

and references in this section to the Secretary of State are to the Secretary of State acting in person.

2D Jurisdiction: review of certain naturalisation and citizenship decisions

(1) Subsection (2) applies in relation to any decision of the Secretary of State which—
- (a) is either—
  - (i) a refusal to issue a certificate of naturalisation under section 6 of the British Nationality Act 1981 to an applicant under that section, or
  - (ii) a refusal to grant an application of the kind mentioned in section 41A of that Act (applications to register an adult or young person as a British citizen etc.), and
- (b) is certified by the Secretary of State as a decision that was made wholly or partly in reliance on information which, in the opinion of the Secretary of State, should not be made public—
  - (i) in the interests of national security,
  - (ii) in the interests of the relationship between the United Kingdom and another country, or
  - (iii) otherwise in the public interest.

(2) The applicant to whom the decision relates may apply to the Special Immigration Appeals Commission to set aside the decision.

(3) In determining whether the decision should be set aside, the Commission must apply the principles which would be applied in judicial review proceedings.

(4) If the Commission decides that the decision should be set aside, it may make any such order, or give any such relief, as may be made or given in judicial review proceedings."

"Norwich Pharmacal" and similar jurisdictions

13 Disclosure proceedings

(1) This section applies where, by way of civil proceedings, a person ("A") seeks the disclosure of information by another person ("B") on the grounds that—
- (a) wrongdoing by another person ("C") has, or may have, occurred,

(b) B was involved with the carrying out of the wrongdoing (whether innocently or not), and

(c) the disclosure is reasonably necessary to enable redress to be obtained or a defence to be relied on in connection with the wrongdoing.

(2) A court may not, in exercise of its residual disclosure jurisdiction, order the disclosure of information sought (whether that disclosure would be to A or to another person) if the information is sensitive information.

(3) "Sensitive information" means information—
   (a) held by an intelligence service,
   (b) obtained from, or held on behalf of, an intelligence service,
   (c) derived in whole or part from information obtained from, or held on behalf of, an intelligence service,
   (d) relating to an intelligence service, or
   (e) specified or described in a certificate issued by the Secretary of State, in relation to the proceedings, as information which B should not be ordered to disclose.

(4) The Secretary of State may issue a certificate under subsection (3)(e) only if the Secretary of State considers that it would be contrary to the public interest for B to disclose—
   (a) the information,
   (b) whether the information exists, or
   (c) whether B has the information.

(5) For the purposes of subsection (4) a disclosure is contrary to the public interest if it would cause damage—
   (a) to the interests of national security, or
   (b) to the interests of the international relations of the United Kingdom.

(6) In this section—
   "enactment" means an enactment whenever passed or made and includes an enactment contained in—
      (a) an Act of the Scottish Parliament,
      (b) Northern Ireland legislation, or
      (c) a Measure or Act of the National Assembly for Wales,
   "Her Majesty's forces" has the same meaning as in the Armed Forces Act 2006,
   "information" includes—
      (a) information contained in any form of document or stored in any other way, and
      (b) alleged information,
   "intelligence service" means—
      (a) the Security Service,
      (b) the Secret Intelligence Service,
      (c) the Government Communications Headquarters, or
      (d) any part of Her Majesty's forces, or of the Ministry of Defence, which engages in intelligence activities,
   "obtained" means obtained directly or indirectly,

"residual disclosure jurisdiction" means any jurisdiction to order the disclosure of information which is not specifically conferred as such a jurisdiction by or under an enactment.

(7) This section—
    (a) enables the Secretary of State to issue a certificate under subsection (3)(e) where the Secretary of State is B as it enables the Secretary of State to issue such a certificate where another person is B, and
    (b) does not restrict any other right or privilege that the Secretary of State can claim in order to resist an application for the disclosure of information.

14 Review of certification

(1) Where the Secretary of State has issued a certificate under section 13(3)(e) in relation to proceedings, any party to the proceedings may apply to the relevant court to set aside the decision on the ground in subsection (2).

(2) That ground is that the Secretary of State ought not to have determined, in relation to the information specified or described in the certificate, that a disclosure by B as mentioned in section 13(4) would be contrary to the public interest.

(3) In determining whether the decision to issue the certificate should be set aside on the ground in subsection (2), the relevant court must apply the principles which would be applied in judicial review proceedings.

(4) Proceedings arising by virtue of this section are to be treated as section 6 proceedings for the purposes of sections 7 to 11.

(5) Sections 7 to 11 apply in relation to proceedings treated as section 6 proceedings by subsection (4) as if—
    (a) the Secretary of State were the relevant person, and
    (b) the references to the interests of national security in sections 7 and 10 were references to the interests of national security or the interests of the international relations of the United Kingdom.

(6) In this section "relevant court" means—
    (a) if the court seised of the proceedings in relation to which the certificate has been issued is a county court, the High Court,
    (b) if the court seised of those proceedings is the sheriff, the Court of Session, and
    (c) in any other case, the court seised of those proceedings.

PART 3

GENERAL

15 Consequential and transitional etc. provision

(1) Schedules 2 and 3 (which make consequential and transitional provision) have effect.

(2) The Secretary of State may by order made by statutory instrument make such transitional, transitory or saving provision as the Secretary of State considers

appropriate in connection with the coming into force of any provision of this Act.

16 Commencement, extent and short title

(1) Sections 1 to 14 and 15(1) (including Schedules 1 to 3) come into force on such day as the Secretary of State may by order made by statutory instrument appoint; and different days may be appointed for different purposes.

(2) Section 15(2) and this section come into force on the day on which this Act is passed.

(3) Subject to subsection (4), this Act extends to England and Wales, Scotland and Northern Ireland.

(4) In Schedule 2—
   (a) the amendments of the Senior Courts Act 1981 extend to England and Wales only,
   (b) the amendments of the Equality Act 2006 and the Equality Act 2010 extend to England and Wales and Scotland only, and
   (c) the amendment of the Race Relations (Northern Ireland) Order 1997 extends to Northern Ireland only.

(5) This Act may be cited as the Justice and Security Act 2012.

SCHEDULES

SCHEDULE 1

Section 1(7)

THE INTELLIGENCE AND SECURITY COMMITTEE

Tenure of office

1 (1) Subject as follows, a person appointed as a member of the ISC during a Parliament holds office for the duration of that Parliament.

   (2) A member of the ISC vacates office if—

   (a) the person ceases to be a member of the House of Parliament by virtue of which the person is a member of the ISC,

   (b) the person becomes a Minister of the Crown, or

   (c) a resolution for the person's removal is passed in the House of Parliament by virtue of which the person is a member of the ISC.

   (3) A member of the ISC may resign at any time by notice given to—

   (a) the Chair of the ISC, or

   (b) in the case of the member who is the Chair of the ISC, the Speaker of the House of Parliament by virtue of which the person is a member of the ISC.

   (4) A person who ceases to be a member of the ISC is eligible for reappointment.

   (5) Section 1(2) does not affect the validity of anything done between the occurrence of a vacancy and the vacancy being filled.

   (6) Anything which, immediately before the end of a Parliament, is in the process of being done or omitted to be done by or in relation to the ISC may be continued by or in relation to the ISC in the new Parliament.

   (7) Anything done or omitted to be done by or in relation to the ISC in a Parliament (or treated as so done or omitted) is, if in force or effective immediately before the end of that Parliament, to have effect as if done or omitted by or in relation to the ISC in the new Parliament so far as that is required for continuing its effect in that Parliament.

Procedure

2 (1) The ISC may determine its own procedure; but this is subject to sub-paragraphs (2) to (5).

   (2) If on any matter there is an equality of voting among the members of the ISC, the Chair of the ISC has a second or casting vote.

   (3) The Chair of the ISC may appoint another member of the ISC to act, in the Chair's absence, as the chair of the ISC at any meeting of it.

(4) A person appointed under sub-paragraph (3) does not enjoy the right conferred on the Chair of the ISC by sub-paragraph (2).

(5) The quorum of the ISC is three.

Access to information

3 (1) If the Director-General of the Security Service, the Chief of the Secret Intelligence Service or the Director of the Government Communications Headquarters is asked by the ISC in the exercise of its functions to disclose any information, then, as to the whole or any part of the information which is sought, that person must either—
  (a) arrange for it to be made available to the ISC subject to and in accordance with a memorandum of understanding under section 2, or
  (b) inform the ISC that the information cannot be disclosed because the Secretary of State has decided that it should not be disclosed.

(2) If the ISC in the exercise of its functions asks a government department or any part of a government department to disclose information, then, as to the whole or any part of the information which is sought, the relevant Minister of the Crown must either—
  (a) arrange for it to be made available to the ISC subject to and in accordance with a memorandum of understanding under section 2, or
  (b) inform the ISC that the information cannot be disclosed because the Minister of the Crown has decided that it should not be disclosed.

(3) A Minister of the Crown may decide under sub-paragraph (1)(b) or (2)(b) that information should not be disclosed only if the Minister considers that—
  (a) it is—
    (i) sensitive information (as defined in paragraph 4), and
    (ii) information which, in the interests of national security, should not be disclosed to the ISC, or
  (b) it is information of such a nature that, if the Minister were requested to produce it before a Departmental Select Committee of the House of Commons, the Minister would consider (on grounds which were not limited to national security) it proper not to do so.

(4) The disclosure of information to the ISC in accordance with sub-paragraph (1) is to be regarded for the purposes of the Security Service Act 1989 or the Intelligence Services Act 1994 as necessary for the proper discharge of the functions of the Security Service, the Secret Intelligence Service or (as the case may be) the Government Communications Headquarters.

(5) In this paragraph "relevant Minister of the Crown", in relation to a request for information, means—
  (a) such Minister of the Crown as is identified, for the purposes of requests of that description, in a memorandum of understanding under section 2, or
  (b) if no Minister of the Crown is so identified, any Minister of the Crown.

Sensitive information

4 The following information is sensitive information for the purposes of paragraph 3(3)(a)—
   (a) information which might lead to the identification of, or provide details of, sources of information, other assistance or operational methods available to—
      (i) the Security Service,
      (ii) the Secret Intelligence Service,
      (iii) the Government Communications Headquarters, or
      (iv) any part of a government department, or any part of Her Majesty's forces, which is engaged in intelligence or security activities,
   (b) information about particular operations which have been, are being or are proposed to be undertaken in pursuance of any of the functions of the persons mentioned in paragraph (a)(i) to (iv),
   (c) information provided by, or by an agency of, the Government of a country or territory outside the United Kingdom where that Government does not consent to the disclosure of the information.

SCHEDULE 2

Section 15(1)

CONSEQUENTIAL PROVISION

PART 1

OVERSIGHT OF INTELLIGENCE AND SECURITY ACTIVITIES

Intelligence Services Act 1994 (c. 13)

1 The following provisions of the Intelligence Services Act 1994 are repealed—
   (a) section 10 (the Intelligence and Security Committee),
   (b) section 11(1)(c) (the definition of "Minister of the Crown"), and
   (c) Schedule 3 (further provision about the Intelligence and Security Committee).

Northern Ireland Act 1998 (c. 47)

2 In section 69B(1)(a) of the Northern Ireland Act 1998 (disregarding notice of the Northern Ireland Human Rights Commission where it requires the disclosure of sensitive information) for "paragraph 4 of Schedule 3 to the Intelligence Services Act 1994 (c. 13)" substitute "paragraph 4 of Schedule 1 to the Justice and Security Act 2012".

Regulation of Investigatory Powers Act 2000 (c. 23)

3 In section 60(1) of the Regulation of Investigatory Powers Act 2000 (duty to disclose documents and provide information to the Intelligence Services Commissioner) for "section 59" substitute "sections 59 and 59A".

Equality Act 2006 (c. 3)

4   In paragraph 14(1)(a) of Schedule 2 to the Equality Act 2006 (disregarding notice of the Commission for Equality and Human Rights where it requires the disclosure of sensitive information) for "paragraph 4 of Schedule 3 to the Intelligence Services Act 1994 (c. 13)" substitute "paragraph 4 of Schedule 1 to the Justice and Security Act 2012".

PART 2

CLOSED MATERIAL PROCEDURE

Judicature (Northern Ireland) Act 1978 (c. 23)

5   (1) Section 62 of the Judicature (Northern Ireland) Act 1978 (trial with and without jury) is amended as follows.

(2) In subsection (2) —
  (a) at the end of paragraph (c), the word "or" is repealed, and
  (b) after paragraph (c) insert—
    "(ca) will involve section 6 proceedings; or".

(3) After subsection (4) insert—

  "(4A) An action in the High Court which by virtue of subsection (1) or (4) is being, or is to be, tried with a jury may, at any stage in the proceedings, be tried without a jury if the court concerned—
    (a) is of opinion that the action involves, or will involve, section 6 proceedings; and
    (b) in its discretion orders the action to be tried without a jury.

  (4B) Where the court makes an order under subsection (4A)(b), it may make such other orders as it considers appropriate (including an order dismissing the jury)."

(4) After subsection (7) insert—

  "(8) In this section "section 6 proceedings" has the meaning given by section 11(1) of the Justice and Security Act 2012 (certain civil proceedings in which closed material applications may be made)."

Senior Courts Act 1981 (c. 54)

6   (1) Section 69 of the Senior Courts Act 1981 (trial by jury) is amended as follows.

(2) In subsection (1), at the end, insert "or unless the court is of opinion that the trial will involve section 6 proceedings".

(3) After subsection (3) insert—

  "(3A) An action in the Queen's Bench Division which by virtue of subsection (1) or (3) is being, or is to be, tried with a jury may, at any stage in the proceedings, be tried without a jury if the court concerned—
    (a) is of opinion that the action involves, or will involve, section 6 proceedings, and
    (b) in its discretion orders the action to be tried without a jury.

(3B) Where the court makes an order under subsection (3A)(b), it may make such other orders as it considers appropriate (including an order dismissing the jury)."

(4) In subsection (4) for "(3)" substitute "(3B)".

(5) After subsection (5) insert—

"(6) In this section "section 6 proceedings" has the meaning given by section 11(1) of the Justice and Security Act 2012 (certain civil proceedings in which closed material applications may be made)."

Special Immigration Appeals Commission Act 1997 (c. 68)

7 (1) The Special Immigration Appeals Commission Act 1997 is amended as follows.

(2) After section 6 (appointment of person to represent appellant's interests) insert—

"6A Procedure in relation to jurisdiction under sections 2C and 2D

(1) Sections 5 and 6 apply in relation to reviews under section 2C or 2D as they apply in relation to appeals under section 2 or 2B.

(2) Accordingly—
 (a) references to appeals are to be read as references to reviews (and references to appeals under section 2 or 2B are to be read as references to reviews under section 2C or 2D), and
 (b) references to an appellant are to be read as references to an applicant under section 2C(2) or (as the case may be) 2D(2)."

(3) After section 7(2) (appeals from the Commission) insert—

"(2A) Where the Commission has made a final determination of a review under section 2C or 2D, any party to the review may bring an appeal against that determination to the appropriate appeal court."

Race Relations (Northern Ireland) Order 1997 (S.I. 1997/869 (N.I.6))

8 In Article 54A of the Race Relations (Northern Ireland) Order 1997 (claims under Article 20A in immigration cases), at the end, insert—

"(6) This Article applies in relation to reviews under section 2D of the 1997 Act as it applies in relation to appeals under that Act."

Regulation of Investigatory Powers Act 2000 (c. 23)

9 (1) Section 18 of the Regulation of Investigatory Powers Act 2000 (exclusion of intercepted communications etc. from legal proceedings: exceptions) is amended as follows.

(2) In subsection (1)—
 (a) at the end of paragraph (e), the word "or" is repealed, and
 (b) after paragraph (f) insert ", or
  "(g) any section 6 proceedings within the meaning given by section 11(1) of the Justice and Security Act 2012

(certain civil proceedings in which closed material applications may be made)."

(3) In subsection (2) —
    (a) in the opening words, for "(f)" substitute "(g)",
    (b) in paragraph (a) —
        (i) in sub-paragraph (i), after "appellant" insert "or (as the case may be) applicant",
        (ii) in sub-paragraph (ii), after "appellant" insert "or applicant", and
        (iii) at the end, the word "or" is repealed, and
    (c) after paragraph (b) insert —
        "(c) in the case of proceedings falling within paragraph (g) where the only relevant person is the Secretary of State, to —
            (i) a person, other than the Secretary of State, who is or was a party to the proceedings; or
            (ii) any person who for the purposes of the proceedings (but otherwise than by virtue of appointment as a special advocate) represents a person falling within sub-paragraph (i); or
        (d) in the case of proceedings falling within paragraph (g) where the Secretary of State is not the only relevant person or is not a relevant person but is a party to the proceedings, to —
            (i) a person, other than the relevant person concerned or the Secretary of State, who is or was a party to the proceedings; or
            (ii) any person who for the purposes of the proceedings (but otherwise than by virtue of appointment as a special advocate) represents a person falling within sub-paragraph (i)."

(4) After subsection (2) insert —

    "(2A) In subsection (2)(c) and (d) "relevant person", in relation to proceedings falling within subsection (1)(g), has the meaning given by section 11(1) of the Justice and Security Act 2012."

Equality Act 2010 (c. 15)

10   In section 115 of the Equality Act 2010 (immigration cases), at the end, insert —

    "(8) This section applies in relation to reviews under section 2D of the Special Immigration Appeals Commission Act 1997 as it applies in relation to appeals under the immigration provisions."

SCHEDULE 3

Section 15(1)

TRANSITIONAL PROVISION

PART 1

OVERSIGHT OF INTELLIGENCE AND SECURITY ACTIVITIES

1   (1) The persons who, immediately before the coming into force of section 1(1), were members of the previous Intelligence and Security Committee become, on the coming into force of section 1(1), members of the new Intelligence and Security Committee.

(2) The person who, immediately before the coming into force of section 1(1), was the Chairman of the previous Intelligence and Security Committee becomes, on the coming into force of section 1(1), the Chair of the new Intelligence and Security Committee.

(3) The new Intelligence and Security Committee may have access to documents or other information provided or belonging to the previous Intelligence and Security Committee.

(4) In this paragraph—

"the new Intelligence and Security Committee" means the Intelligence and Security Committee established under section 1 of this Act,

"the previous Intelligence and Security Committee" means the Intelligence and Security Committee established under section 10 of the Intelligence Services Act 1994.

PART 2

CLOSED MATERIAL PROCEDURE

2   Sections 6 to 11, and paragraphs 5, 6 and 9 of Schedule 2 (other than paragraph 9(3)(b)(i) and (ii)), apply in relation to proceedings begun, but not finally determined, before the coming into force of section 6 (in addition to proceedings begun on or after the coming into force of that section).

3   (1) The first time after the passing of this Act that rules of court are made in exercise of the powers conferred by sections 6 to 11 in relation to proceedings in England and Wales or in Northern Ireland before a court of a particular description, the rules (together with any related rules of court) may be made by the Lord Chancellor instead of by the person who would otherwise make them.

(2) Before making rules of court under sub-paragraph (1), the Lord Chancellor must consult—

   (a) in relation to rules applicable to proceedings in England and Wales, the Lord Chief Justice of England and Wales, and

   (b) in relation to rules applicable to proceedings in Northern Ireland, the Lord Chief Justice of Northern Ireland.

(3) But the Lord Chancellor is not required to undertake any other consultation before making the rules.

(4) A requirement to consult under sub-paragraph (2) may be satisfied by consultation that took place wholly or partly before the passing of this Act.

(5) Rules of court made by the Lord Chancellor under sub-paragraph (1)—
  (a) must be laid before Parliament, and
  (b) if not approved by a resolution of each House before the end of 40 days beginning with the day on which they were made, cease to have effect at the end of that period.

(6) In determining that period of 40 days no account is to be taken of any time during which Parliament is dissolved or prorogued or during which both Houses are adjourned for more than 4 days.

(7) If rules cease to have effect in accordance with sub-paragraph (5)—
  (a) that does not affect anything done in previous reliance on the rules, and
  (b) sub-paragraph (1) applies again as if the rules had not been made.

(8) The following provisions do not apply to rules of court made by the Lord Chancellor under this paragraph—
  (a) section 3(6) of the Civil Procedure Act 1997 (Parliamentary procedure for civil procedure rules),
  (b) section 56(1), (2) and (4) of the Judicature (Northern Ireland) Act 1978 (statutory rules procedure).

(9) Until the coming into force of section 85 of the Courts Act 2003, the reference in sub-paragraph (8)(a) to section 3(6) of the Civil Procedure Act 1997 is to be read as a reference to section 3(2) of that Act.

(10) In this paragraph "related rules of court" means rules of court that—
  (a) are contained in the same instrument as the rules mentioned in sub-paragraph (1), and
  (b) relate specifically to the same kind of proceedings as those rules.

PART 3

"NORWICH PHARMACAL" AND SIMILAR JURISDICTIONS

4   Sections 13 and 14 apply in relation to proceedings begun, but not finally determined, before the coming into force of section 13 (in addition to proceedings begun on or after the coming into force of that section).

Justice and Security Bill [HL]

A

BILL

To provide for oversight of the Security Service, the Secret Intelligence Service, the Government Communications Headquarters and other activities relating to intelligence or security matters; to provide for closed material procedure in relation to certain civil proceedings; to prevent the making of certain court orders for the disclosure of sensitive information; and for connected purposes.

Lord Wallace of Tankerness

Ordered to be Printed, 28th May 2012

© Parliamentary copyright House of Lords 2012

This publication may be reproduced under the terms of the Parliamentary Click-Use Licence, available online through The National Archives website at www.nationalarchives.gov.uk/information-management/our-services/parliamentary-licence-information.htm Enquiries to The National Archives, Kew, Richmond, Surrey, TW9 4DU; email: psi@nationalarchives.gsi.gov.uk

PUBLISHED BY AUTHORITY OF THE HOUSE OF LORDS
LONDON — THE STATIONERY OFFICE LIMITED
Printed in the United Kingdom by The Stationery Office Limited
£4.00

ISBN 978-0-10-843375-7